From the Outhouse to the White House

White House

Randolph Lancaster

From the Outhouse to the White House
Copyright © 2025 by Randolph Lancaster

ISBN: 979-8894791494 (sc)
ISBN: 979-8894791500 (e)

The Reading Glass Books
BOOKS

The Reading Glass Books
1-888-420-3050
www.readingglassbooks.com
production@readingglassbooks.com

From the Outhouse to the White House.

I decided to write this book because of what I've been hearing on the news about the two-tiered justice system in America. I have long since believed that this two-tiered justice system is all about the long-standing corruption by money and power within our so-called justice system. This two-tiered justice system in America has been going on for the last 60 years, of which I am aware. The fact is, what I am stating in this book is easy to prove. You just need to do your research. Almost everything that I talk about in this book can be proven with a little research. However, I thought I would share with you a few news articles with the link and/ or sources of those news articles to get you started.

In this book, I wanted to reflect on the 60's, ...70's, ...and other News and Events leading up until now. Tell you what it was like to be a kid back then and what was going on at the time in America's Society from my perspective. This is my story. My criminal story. Plus a few other stories of some criminals along the way. The news, events, and stories in this book shed light on our brutal and corrupt system in America. These past experiences and events have led to my doubts and beliefs in America's Justice System overall.

I can tell you honestly that I am no expert; but the choices we make in life WILL define us. Whether the choices you make are good or bad. Your choices will still define YOU. No matter who you are, whatever you do or wherever you go! In Life, ...GOD is watching Every move you make, and HE knows what is in your heart. Throughout everything that I have been through in my life, I do believe in GOD. I ask those who read this book to have integrity and choose to do the right thing even when no one is watching. I just don't want to see people trash their lives the way I have mine. With that bit of advice, just maybe you will not crush your dreams and mess up your life like I had crushed mine. Again, I am no expert, and I have led a strange life. A little like the Twilight Zone. And here is my story.....

Chapter One

Early in Life

I was born in Topeka, Kansas In 1948. My parents got divorced when I was two years old, I moved with my mother to a place called Commerce City, CO. Growing up in Commerce City for me was rough and everybody was poor in the 1950's. Minimum wage was .90 cents per hour. In the 1960's, minimum wage was $1.25 per hour. One week's wages would pay for one month's rent. When I was 5 years old, my sister got married. Their rent for her and her husband was $35 per month for a NICE apartment. That same apartment would cost you $1250 or more per month nowadays here in Colorado. Inflation and the cost of living now make me wish we were back in those days of the 50's.

Growing up in Commerce City, there were quite a few experiences in my life that had an impact on me. These experiences helped to shape me into the man I am today when it comes to how I treat my fellow man. One memory was when my mother helped to save a baby's life. We had a woman show up one day at our house unexpectedly. We didn't know the woman. We had never seen her before.

She was young, about 18 years old or so, with blonde, messy, scraggly looking hair. She was scared and upset; and she had a baby in her arms. Come to find out the baby she held in her arms was hers. She asked my mother for help because the baby wasn't breathing. My mother grabbed a blanket and laid the baby on our table. My mother knew that this baby needed a doctor's care. The next thing I knew, we were all in the car. My mother, the young woman, the baby, and myself. The only doctors for miles around at that time were Flackster and Schumann. We rushed to get that baby to them. They saved that baby's life! My mom's quick thinking saved that baby's life!

The next day my mother had another knock at our door, and it was the young woman. Her appearance had changed so much from the day previously. She was so happy. My mother invited her to come in and she thanked my mother for saving her child's life. I don't remember their names. I am sure my mother asked her, and names were exchanged. I just remember the impact it had on me. It makes me quite emotional when I think of that memory because my mother could have chosen to not help that young mother but that was not who MY mother was. She cared for people, and she did not judge them.

When I was about 5 years old, we were in Topeka Kansas. This was around 1953. We were going to the Coffee Cup Cafe. I remember it sat right on the corner of the street. It was a classic diner where people went to meet each other, significant others or friends. It had a great big coffee cup on the top of the roof with neon lights in every window. It was a popular, hit place that everyone went to. You could get your coffee there for $0.05, with free refills.

I remember the temperature that day was about 70°. As we were headed to the diner, I saw a man who was crossing the street. He was wearing a heavy trench coat and a hat. The weather was warm, and I was curious as to why he was wearing a coat and not a regular coat, a heavy coat. Then I noticed the color of his skin. His skin was white. At that point in time, I had never seen a person known as an albino before. My mother scolded me for looking at the man. I just stared. I didn't know any better. I was just curious because the weather was warm and here is this man wearing a coat, and not just any regular coat. A heavy coat at that. I turned to look around and looked him in the eyes to let him know that I met him no harm and I recall seeing gauze all over the man's face and nose, I was able to see his eyes, which were brown. His kind eyes looked back at me and let me know that he knew I meant no disrespect or harm.

When I went into the cafe with my mother, we were waiting for a table. She started talking to the waitresses and they were talking about the albino man. One lady said he came in every once in a while, and works at a camera shop. She said he was known as an albino and that he couldn't stand sunlight or to be near any bright lights at all. I instantly felt sorry for him and thought it sad that he was not able to go out to play. That was in my 5-year-old mentality. My mother told me that day that I am no better than anyone else and nobody else is better than me. We are all equal. I have lived by that rule all of my life. I have never chosen my friends or my enemies by the color of their skin.

When I was in the second grade, two things impacted my life. One, my stepfather started beating on me. Two, I started attending Monaco Elementary School where I had a teacher by the name of Miss Wilder. One day, Miss Wilder and I were talking about people, and she said to me that if you judge people by the color of their skin, what is next? Tall or short? Skinny or fat? People that think like this need to read the book the Elephant Man about John Merrick. That resonated with me because of what my mother had taught me a few years before.

School for me was my escape from my reality at home. I received daily beatings from my stepfather. I loved my mother, but I hated my stepfather. The beatings from my step-father quit around the fourth grade but it had such an impact on me that I was lost.

I went to Topeka, KS, with my mother, my stepfather, and my mother's mother. My grandmother was ill, so we took a trip back to Topeka, KS, to their house. This was when I was really young. In their room, over the main room, they had a big, old pot-bellied stove. All the walls were covered in soot—hardly any place to even sit down. It was so bad. There was a back porch, and on the back porch, they had a stump of wood, a hammer, and bags of walnuts. When they didn't want me around, I would go out back and bust the walnuts, then bring the nuts inside.

Later, I'd go back inside and tell my mom I had to use the bathroom. When my grandma wasn't looking, my mom would take toilet paper out of her purse and sneak it to me. I'd go out to the outhouse because, well, these people used newspapers and old magazines for taking care of business. Afterward, I'd have to sneak the toilet paper back to my mom so as not to embarrass anyone.

Yeah, a lot of people had outhouses back then, even in Denver, CO. For example, on 3740-something Washington Street, near the slaughterhouse, a lot of those old houses had outhouses. Some relatives of ours lived in that area. At night, if you had to go out, it was easy to find the outhouse—just follow the stench. Oh, it was terrible back then.

Things were tough when I was young. Nobody had any money in the '50s. Everyone was flat broke. I remember when I was about 9 or 10 years old, I'd hustle two cent pop bottles and buy a nickel candy bar. That was my first hustle. I'd take the pop bottles and walk up to the little store to cash them in.

One day, I was heading to the store—little corner stores were common back then. A friend of mine lived catty-corner from the store. He came up to me and asked, "What's going on? What are you doing?" He told me he was the youngest in a family of four boys, with three older brothers. Next door lived a girl named Susan Struna, who had three older sisters. They lived right next to each other.

Russell, my friend, was telling me how they'd been teasing each other. He called them "Struna turds," and they ran back inside to tell their parents. Nowadays, people would get all worked up over something like that, thinking it's racist or something. But back then, it was just kids being kids. The Struna kids came back out and started calling Russell "rubber ass." It was all in good fun.

Chapter Two

The Loris Guzman Story

I was about 13 years old and attending Adams City Junior High School at the time. Whoever made up my schedule had to be crazy because I'd have to run from one building to another, and I had to do it all within 5 minutes. You know what I'm saying? So, anyhow, I was running through the buildings, but I knew Dolores Guzman. I first started talking to her because I have a sister named Dolores, and we talked about that. She was really a nice person—kind, considerate, and of Mexican descent. She didn't talk much, just a little bit, but whenever I came through, she'd always be smiling, and I'd smile back at her.

One day, she died. She had to have her leg amputated and didn't last very long after that. The day she died, I was so upset. I went behind the house that I lived in. There was this empty field behind where I live and that is where I cursed GOD and I called him every bad word I could think of. I was mad because of all the people he could have taken that lived around where I lived. And he chose her. I never held her hand or kissed her lips. She was my friend and I value friendship a lot. A lot of people use that term very loosely.

In 7th grade, I attended Adams City Junior High School. Later, we moved into a bigger home, and I went to Kearney Junior High for 8th and 9th grade. I was in 8th grade when we moved. In English class, I noticed the parking lot was full of scoopers coming in around 1:00 PM.

I attended Adams City High School for 10th and 11th grade. That's when I started getting into more trouble. I didn't want to be home, and I wasn't getting any guidance. In my senior year, I went to Northglenn High School. At the beginning of the year, I didn't want to stay where I was.

Life was tough when I was a kid. Everybody was struggling in the 50s and 60s. No one had any money. For example, the meat truck would always have extra meat they needed to get rid of by the end of the day, so they'd sell it cheap. Everyone was stealing just to get by—even the cops. It's hard to believe, but it's true. It was everywhere, so I didn't think much of it.

The was around the time of the infamous Burglars in Blue scandal in Denver.

The Happy Cat Tavern was hit for $2,000 and two cases of whisky. From the Reese House restaurant, $4,000 was stolen. The U.S. Loan Co. Lost $7,250. There were scores of others, and finally $40,000 was swiped from a Safeway supermarket on Denver's south side in one of the biggest thefts in the city's history. Denver screamed for the police to do something.

The cops, it turned out, already had. No fewer than 35 of Denver's police force had been fingered as the actual burglars. In all, over a seven-year period, the burglars in blue had committed at least 129 crimes.

Denver's burgling cops were well organized and enjoyed obvious advantages. They cased jobs from police cars, returned at night to steal while lookouts monitored the police radio for alarm calls. Once the burglaries were discovered, the same policemen came back officially to investigate, were able to destroy any leftover evidence. In one case, an insurance company investigator discovered a pair of policeman's trousers near a burglary scene. Two city detectives confiscated the evidence ; the pants disappeared forever.

In the Safeway burglary, the police knew that extra cash was in the store. The crooked cops carefully surveyed the one-story, yellow brick building during the day. A few nights later, three policemen jimmied the aluminum front door. A police car stopped across the street as lookout; one of the three burglars remained by the store window to watch for a flashing-headlight danger signal. At the safe, his two companions worked with a carborundum wheel, cooled it with cartons of milk. In 90 minutes the safe was cracked.

As the disgraced cops paraded before his disgusted gaze, at the State Capitol, Colorado's Democratic Governor Stephen McNichols, a onetime FBI man, explained that the ring had sprung from a single group in the south Denver district. When gang members were transferred to other districts, new members were recruited.

There were few failures—but one of them led to the burglars' downfall. Cruising one night in April 1960, Patrolman John D. Bates saw burglars leave a 17th Street coffee shop. When Bates chased the getaway car, a safe fell out of the trunk; the man who came back to retrieve it turned out to be a policeman. Bates told his story to Chief James E. Childers, passed on department rumors that a dozen policemen were cracking safes. He was ordered to see a psychiatrist. When the psychiatrist reported Bates was eminently sane and was probably telling the truth, the police department began an investigation. It lasted almost a year, and it was found that the corruption spread beyond Denver's city limits. The sheriff of neighboring Adams County was arrested, and five sheriff's officers were nabbed in adjacent Arapahoe County.

Said Governor McNichols: "We think we have the hard core:" Chief Childers, under severe criticism for his laxity, resigned, and a top-to-bottom overhaul began. Because the burglars had systematically faked police records, no one was able to say exactly how much had been taken over the years; the Safeway supermarket chain alone estimated it had lost $125,000. With many of its veteran cops in jail, the Denver 778-man police department was hard put to keep up patrols; 28 rookies with only two weeks' experience were rushed into regular duty. But worse than the shortage was the loss of faith that Denver had in its police. When two cops cruised up to a housing project last week, a group of workmen yelled: "We got to lock up our cars. Cops are in the neighborhood."

Big Randy and Little Randy

When I was 16, I got to the point where I started doing car washes. It was 25 cents for a wash, rinse, and 5 minutes of time. I figured out how to open the coin box with a bobby pin. It was like that scene in *Happy Days* where you hit the jukebox, and it starts playing music. They were that easy to open.

One day, when I was in court, I told my lawyer, "Hey, that guy up there is lying. That cop is lying." My lawyer said, "One will lie and fifty will swear to it." I never thought I'd be able to prove something like that, but now I can. Remember the 50 laureates who said Hunter Bidens laptop was Russian disinformation? Fifty of them lied. Now, it's proven. This actually affected the 2020 election. That's how corrupt these people are. I'll include more about this later in the book.

When I was a kid, there was the "Big Randy and Little Randy" story. I was Little Randy. My cousin, who lived across the street, was named Randy Wells. His father was Clifford's brother, so he got treated really well, while I got treated like dirt. I ran around with him and got into a lot of trouble. My mom would always ask, "Is this Big Randy or Little Randy?" Sometimes, she'd say, "Which one? Big Randy or Little Randy?" And sometimes, it was both of us. It was a lot of trouble back then

I was in Mr. Addison's 8th grade English class when the president of the United States J.F.K. was shot. The school buses showed up in the middle of the afternoon and closed the whole school.

When I was 14, I was in Mr. Vito's class. He was my 8th-grade history teacher. He wore a suit, was a little heavy-set, and Italian. When the class first started, and the students were noisy, he would say, "Shut your face," trying to sound like a mobster. It was funny how he set everyone straight. "Quit talking," he'd say. He taught world history and American history and was a very good teacher. He taught us how communism, socialism, and Nazism had failed in the past.

Like I said earlier in this book about growing up with a lot of army kids, one day in class, one of the army kids had these other kids jammed up in a corner. These kids thought they were better than anyone else and were sticking up for communism and socialism. When they got jammed up, they started yelling, "Freedom! Freedom of speech! Peace, brother!" The army kids let them off the hook that time. Their fathers were fighting for this country.

The reason I'm telling this story is that socialism, communism, fascism, and Marxist Nazis failed in the past and will fail in the future. This needs to be taught. There's no free lunch; you have to work for what you get. Even at a young age, kids should think about what they want to become. You can become whatever you want in this country, but it takes hard work and the right schooling. Only in America can you do this. In other countries, the government tells you what to do, where to do it, and even what to cook and when to cook it. That's not the America I want to live in. If you like that, keep your head in the sand and your *** in the air for another 60 years. And that's the end of that.

The Three Kings

This story is about the Three Kings: JFK, MLK, and RFK. Camelot, the legendary castle of King Arthur, was supposed to represent truth, justice, and the American way. But the Three Kings' legacy is complicated.

When I was 18, I was living with my father and working on a trash truck. One night, I went to a party that lasted until the early morning. My friends went across the street, kicked in the door of a liquor store, and came back with the liquor. I was inside sleeping when it happened. When I woke up and saw what they did, I just laughed and went home. The next day, I was arrested and charged with cheering on the burglary. I couldn't make bond, so I was sent to jail. My lawyer came to see me one morning and told me that by not reporting the burglary, I was just as guilty.

While I was in jail, I heard people saying it was better to rape, kill, or molest little kids than to commit burglary. I asked my lawyer why those crimes got less time than burglary or armed robbery. He said, "If you were a child molester, I could argue the girl was promiscuous. If it was rape, I could claim self-defense. But burglary? There's no defense for burglary." He was basically telling me that burglary was treated worse than those other crimes.

While I was in jail in Topeka, KS, there was no TV, but you could listen to the radio. I heard on the news that Martin Luther King Jr. was caught cheering on a rape, and the FBI had released the audio. The government has had this recording for 50 years and chose to hide it until January 31, 2027.

In 1968, I was sentenced to Lansing Prison for not reporting the burglary of the liquor store. I got 5 to 10 years. At the same time, a legislator named Tom Kidwell was being tried for the first-degree murder of his wife, who was shot four times in the heart. He was supposed to serve life imprisonment but got an appeal on a technicality. There was even an article published about his trial in Time magazine:

Friday, Dec. 29, 1967
Trials: Reliving a Murder

In a Topeka, Kans., courtroom last week, the lights were flicked off and judge and jury sat enthralled as a deadly serious story began to unfold on TV screens in front of them. The central figure. Thomas Kidwell, 47, had already been convicted of the murder of his promiscuous wife—although he could not remember much about what had happened before he was found in his wrecked car with her nude body on the floor.

At his first trial last February, the prosecution offered a compelling reconstruction. Kidwell was angry at his wife because she wanted an annulment of the year-old marriage. They argued and took a drive. Police witnesses then testified that Kidwell's wife had been shot four times in the heart either after or before he had intercourse with her.

Afterward, the prosecution version continued, Kidwell shot himself twice in the chest in a suicide attempt. The first jury believed the prosecution and convicted Kidwell of first-degree murder. But at last week's second trial, granted because of errors committed at the first, the essential ingredient was something new—an hour-long video tape of Kidwell reliving the murder under the influence of a drug.

In the Skin. Video tape has only just begun its legal career (TIME, Dec. 22), and its Topeka appearance was apparently the second time that one has ever been viewed in court by a judge in the U.S. But the tape is not likely to be surpassed soon for dramatic impact. In preparation for the second trial, Kid-well's lawyer had sent him to the nearby Menninger Clinic in the hope that he would tell doctors there a clearer story about the murder night than he had yet told anyone else. Psychiatrist Joseph Satten, chief of Menninger's law and psychiatry division, decided to try sodium amobarbital, which, though not a truth drug, can help a patient relive a traumatic experience he is unconsciously trying to avoid. Dr. Satten also decided to put the results on video tape for a study of criminals that the clinic was in the process of making.

The prosecution, amazed by what the tape showed, asked the judge to take the highly unusual step of showing it to the jury as the trial's first piece of business. There, on tape, was Kidwell, lying on a couch in an undershirt and slacks. As the drug took hold, he was instructed to begin counting backward from 100. When the count faltered, he was guided by questions from Dr. Satten until he was obviously back with his wife in the murder car, apparently reliving what had happened. He and she "were having a lot of fun," he said. Then, he remembered, she started talking about a former husband's sexual prowess. "A big man in bed," mumbled Kidwell. "Couldn't support his kids, that son of a bitch."

Suddenly, he sucked in his breath and grabbed at his chest. To those seeing Kidwell's reaction on tape, it seemed plain that he was re-experiencing being shot by his wife. Swearing with pain, he forgave her ("It ain't hurt nothing, it's in the skin"), then cursed her. Finally, his jumbled words conveyed that he had got the gun and shot her.

Unconscious Reporting. The complete story was still somewhat fuzzy, but to anyone seeing the tape, it seemed clear that whatever else may have happened, Kidwell's unconscious was reporting that his wife shot him first. When he saw it during a pretrial screening, the prosecuting attorney decided to reduce the charge to first-degree manslaughter; the defense agreed to plead guilty to that charge. Noting that "I think courts have to use the best devices available," Judge William Carpenter, 35, agreed to allow the tape to be shown to the jury, after which the manslaughter plea was accepted. Kidwell now faces a five-to 30-year sentence (which could be suspended entirely) instead of the life sentence he received at his first trial.

Awed at "the value of the tape in conveying the genuineness of the experience," Dr. Satten noted later that "never in a million years on the witness stand could I have had the eloquence and skill in testifying demonstrated by that tape."

While on sodium amytal, he claimed his wife shot him first and got a plea deal of 5 to 21 years. He was placed in a luxurious mobile home outside the prison walls, while I, a 19-year-old, was behind bars. People said, "Different strokes for different folks. Money talks, and bull **** walks."

In 1968, I heard Martin Luther King was assassinated, while Kidwell was safe in his mobile home. During a prison riot, I was in the Adjustment and Treatment Center. They gassed us, shot us with fire hoses, and beat us. Then they put me in a hole for a week with only a slice of bread, spinach, and water.

In 1969, people were talking about making Martin Luther King Jr. a national holiday. Convicts joked about calling it "Martin Luther King Rape Day" or "James Earl Ray Day." They also called him a communist-loving rapist.

In 1969, there was a race riot, and many people were hurt. That same year, Congressman Ted Kennedy drove his car into a body of water, drowning a woman who wasn't his wife. He got two months in jail, probation, and kept his job. Different strokes for different folks.

In 1971, the legislator and I went to the parole board. I got a year set off, and Kidwell made parole. Better to kill your wife than cheer on a burglary, I guess.

In 1971, there was a prison riot in Attica, NY, where 40 people were killed. The government claimed the convicts had guns, but they didn't. The guards killed 10 of their own people.

Now, this next story is about the Queens. Claudine Longet, a beloved actress, accidentally shot her lover, Spider Sabich, in their Aspen home in 1976. She claimed the gun just "went boom." She served only 30 days in jail. Meanwhile, a woman in Denver County got 60 days for stealing food for her kids. It's worse to steal food in Denver than to kill your lover in Aspen.

Another queen is Patty Hearst. She was charged with armed robbery and kidnapping but served only 22 months because her father had money and influence. President Jimmy Carter commuted her sentence, and Bill Clinton later pardoned her.

On June 7, 1977, Ted Bundy escaped twice from Colorado authorities. He was treated like a celebrity, wearing his own clothes in court, while the rest of us wore orange jumpsuits and chains. He went on to kill more women before being executed.

In 1977, the FBI's surveillance of Martin Luther King Jr. was revealed. The tapes, which include King cheering on a rape, are sealed until January 31 2027. The government hides the truth about the Kennedys and King because it doesn't fit the Camelot narrative.

This is the two-tiered justice system at work. I did 6 1/2 years for cheering on a burglary, while others did less time for rape, murder, and bank robbery.

Riots and Massacres

This next chapter is about riots and massacres. I want to talk about the Attica uprising in 1971, which took place from September

9th to the 13th. The Attica riots involved 1,281 inmates, 74 correctional officers, 550 state troopers, and 42 correctional officers and civilian workers taken hostage. The casualties and losses were devastating: 33 inmates were killed (3 by other inmates), 10 correctional officers were killed, and 5 were wounded during the assault. Shockingly, they were even killing their own people. It was chaos. But that's just how things were in the penitentiary system back then. And, of course, nobody went to jail for it. Why would they?

The prisoners were living in horrific conditions. They spent 14 to 16 hours a day in their cells, their mail was read, their reading materials were restricted, and their visits from family were conducted through a mesh screen. Medical care was disgraceful, the parole system was inadequate, and racism was rampant. That's what this prison was like, and that's what led to the uprising. Yet, nobody faced consequences.

Moving on to the 1980s, I want to share another story. I went to prison in 1980 in Arizona. One day, I was sitting in a holding tank after being booked for robbery. Another guy came in and sat across from me. We nodded at each other.

The guards were furious with this guy they had just brought in. One officer yelled, "Get back over here right now! He yelled because the guy they brought in was nobody to be messed with. Because this guy all he had to do was snap his fingers. The saying goes mess around/mess around and pretty soon you won't be around.

When I first arrived at the prison, they sent me to Alhambra, the intake facility where all prisoners are processed. They gave us IQ tests and told us we should have been scientists or doctors— anything but criminals. It's funny how people assume everyone in prison is stupid, but that's not the case.

While I was in Florence, Arizona, I heard a story about two guards who beat up two inmates. The warden found out and said, "I can't leave you guys out here on the yard because of what you did." Instead of arresting or firing them, they were transferred to a medium-security facility. Five years later, those same guards returned to the prison. One of the inmates they had beaten recognized them and told his friend. They armed themselves, attacked the guards, and killed them in a brutal manner. It was a case of what goes around comes around.

The next story is about Gary Tison who had his three son's break him out of the Arizona State Prison in Florence Arizona. After the escape they went on a killing spree, killing seven or eight people including a baby. They were arrested after a shooting at a road block. The oldest boy was killed while running the road block. Gary Tison died of thirst in the desert. Randy Greenwalt was executed at Florence Arizona, State Prison. The two youngest boys got 40 to 50 Years, They made a movie of this, called The Last Rampage. This is what these hate factories have been making for years.

Next, I want to talk about the New Mexico prison riot in 1980. Thirty-three people were killed, and 200 were injured. Yet, nothing ever happened to those responsible. While I was in prison, I heard they moved a dozen inmates from Santa Fe to Florence because there was no room to house them after the riot.

There's also the Ramos case in Colorado. A prisoner filed a lawsuit against the state and won, but six years later, nothing had changed. The cells were still freezing, with no heat or proper conditions. When I asked what started the lawsuit, they said it was because the state didn't follow through on their promises. It's a rigged system.

In another incident, inmates stripped guards of their clothes, beat them, and tortured them with electric cords and cutting torches. It was brutal, but it was also a form of retribution for the abuse they had endured.

This is how the system works. Guards abuse inmates, and inmates retaliate. It's a cycle of violence that never ends. And the people in power—the cops, judges, DAs, legislators, and senators— they're all complicit. They have immunity, and nothing changes.

In 1985 I was sent to cell house six in the Arizona the hole. My next door neighbor was one of the guys that tortured those two guards, Any how they passed a law a couple of years prior that if

15

you draw blood on a resident. That is what they called us in prison. You would receive 25 years in prison. And they were handing it to those that drew blood. Any how a young guy drew blood and was charged but his daddy was a lawyer and had money. He got the law over turned for his son. But did nothing for the previous one's that got the 25 years. More of the two tier, two faced, chicken shit justice system.

I'll end this chapter by talking about Ruby Ridge, which will be part of the next section on gun charges and massacres.

Gun Charges and Massacres

The Ruby Ridge siege in Idaho began on August 21, 1992, when U.S. Marshals attempted to arrest Randy Weaver, a former U.S. Army Green Beret, on a bench warrant for failing to appear on firearms charges. The standoff lasted 11 days and resulted in tragic consequences.

The Ruby Ridge standoff, a 1992 incident in Idaho, involved a 11-day siege of Randy Weaver's cabin by federal agents, resulting in the deaths of a US Marshal, Weaver's 14-year-old son, and his wife, Vicki Weaver, and the wounding of Weaver and his friend Kevin Harris.

Randy Weaver, a former soldier and hunter, was wanted for failing to appear in court on a weapons charge related to the sale of two illegal sawed-off shotguns to an informant.

Weaver and his family, along with a few associates, refused to surrender, leading to an 11-day standoff with federal agents, including the FBI and the US Marshals.

- Deputy US Marshal William Degan was killed in an exchange of gunfire.
- Randy Weaver's 14-year-old son, Samuel Weaver, was shot in the back and killed by federal agents.
- Weaver's wife, Vicki Weaver, was killed by a sniper while standing in the doorway of their cabin.

- Kevin Harris, a friend of Weaver's, was wounded in the same incident.

Weaver and Harris were initially charged with multiple offenses, but were later acquitted on all major charges, with the jury finding that the original weapons charge was entrapment.

The incident sparked controversy and raised questions about the actions of federal law enforcement, leading to investigations and a US$3.1 million settlement for the Weaver family.

The Ruby Ridge standoff is considered a catalyst for the modern American militia movement, and was cited by Timothy McVeigh as a reason for the Oklahoma City bombing.

FBI sniper Lon Horiuchi fired two shots at armed targets, the first shot hitting Randy Weaver, and the second shot, intended for Kevin Harris, instead killed Vicki Weaver.

The U.S. Department of Justice created a "Ruby Ridge Task Force" to investigate the incident, and the task force concluded that the first shot by Horiuchi met the standard of "objective reasonableness," but the second shot did not

It's interesting to note the contrast in how gun charges are handled. Take Hunter Biden, for example. He was charged with a gun-related offense, but it wasn't until two whistleblowers came forward that the case gained traction. Initially, they were aiming for a 50-year sentence, but that didn't happen. It's a stark reminder of how the system operates differently for different people.

Now, back to Ruby Ridge. During the standoff, law enforcement's actions led to the deaths of several individuals, including Weaver's wife and son. Yet, no one was held accountable. It's the same old story: no consequences for those in power.

Next, let's talk about Waco. The Waco siege happened in 1993 and involved the Branch Davidians. Nearly 80 people, including 17 children, died during the standoff. Again, no one was held responsible. It's a recurring theme: Ruby Ridge, Waco, and countless other incidents where lives are lost, yet no one faces justice.

Here's a more detailed breakdown:

- The Waco Siege: The siege began on February 28, 1993, when the Bureau of Alcohol, Tobacco and Firearms (ATF) raided the Mount Carmel Center, the home of the Branch Davidians led by David Koresh.

- Initial Gunfight: The raid resulted in a gunfight that killed four ATF agents and six Branch Davidians.

- 51-Day Standoff: The FBI took over the situation, and a 51-day standoff ensued.

- Final Assault and Fire: On April 19, 1993, the FBI launched a final assault, using tear gas and tanks, which led to a massive fire that engulfed the compound.

- Casualties: The fire and the events surrounding it resulted in the deaths of 76 Branch Davidians, including Koresh and an estimated 20-28 children.

- Survivors: Nine Branch Davidians escaped the fire

Then came Timothy McVeigh. In 1995, he detonated a truck bomb outside the Alfred P. Murrah Federal Building in Oklahoma City, killing 168 people, including children. McVeigh's actions were a direct response to what he saw as government overreach, particularly in the aftermath of Ruby Ridge and Waco. His attack was a brutal reminder of the consequences of unchecked authority and the cycle of violence it can perpetuate.

On the morning of April 19, 1995, an ex-Army soldier and security guard named Timothy McVeigh parked a rented Ryder truck in front of the Alfred P. Murrah Federal Building in downtown Oklahoma City.

He was about to commit mass murder.

Inside the vehicle was a powerful bomb made out of a deadly cocktail of agricultural fertilizer, diesel fuel, and other chemicals. McVeigh got out, locked the door, and headed towards his getaway car. He ignited one timed fuse, then another.

At precisely 9:02 a.m., the bomb exploded.

Within moments, the surrounding area looked like a war zone. A third of the building had been reduced to rubble, with many floors flattened like pancakes. Dozens of cars were incinerated and more than 300 nearby buildings were damaged or destroyed.

The human toll was still more devastating: 168 souls lost, including 19 children, with several hundred more injured.

These events—Ruby Ridge, Waco, and the Oklahoma City bombing—highlight a disturbing pattern of violence and impunity. People are killed, lives are destroyed, yet those responsible for the initial actions rarely face consequences. It's a system that protects its own while ordinary citizens bear the brunt of its failures.

Personal Stories:

When I was 10 years old, I witnessed something that stuck with me. I went to a little store one day and saw two guys stealing. A little girl, about 5 years old, pointed it out, but no one paid attention. I knew what was happening, but I just turned away. That kind of behavior was everywhere back then.

At 16, I got busted for stealing car parts. My probation officer was William Buckley. He told me he was working as a probation officer to get a law degree. I didn't think much of it at the time, but looking back, I realize that was where my troubles really began.

When I was 19, I was charged with burglary. I spent time in jail in Topeka, Kansas, where I heard about Martin Luther King Jr.'s assassination. Everyone in jail was calling him a "commie-loving rapist. Hoover's FBI had exposed the truth, and it was clear that King's death was part of a larger pattern of systemic injustice.

The System's Failures:

In 1977, I was in prison in Colorado. That's when I saw firsthand how the system operates. Claudia and Patty Hearst were in the news, and I realized how much corruption there was at every level of government. From JFK to Bobby Kennedy to Martin Luther King Jr., the system was rigged to protect the powerful while punishing the vulnerable.

I did 6.5 years for not reporting a burglary, while people like Hunter Biden, Martin Luther King jr. and others involved in far more serious crimes faced little to no consequences. It's a two-tiered system: one for the rich and powerful, and another for the rest of us.

Ruby Ridge, Waco, and Beyond:

The Ruby Ridge and Waco sieges, along with the Oklahoma City bombing, are stark reminders of how violence begets violence. Timothy McVeigh's actions were horrific, but they were also a response to the government's heavy-handed tactics at Ruby Ridge and Waco. The cycle of violence continues because those in power refuse to be held accountable.

Final Thoughts:

This chapter is about exposing the corruption that runs from the outhouse to the White House. It's about the Attica uprising, the Santa Fe prison riot, and the countless other instances where people have been killed, injured, or wronged, yet no one is held responsible.

The system is broken, and it's up to us to demand change. Until then, the cycle of violence and injustice will continue.

Louis Farrakhan and Obama White House Story – Black Supremacy: One Picture Says It All This is the story of how Barack Obama associated with the Black Supremacist leader Louis Farrakhan. The image speaks volumes about the double standards in our society.

When I Was 19 Years Old:

When I was 17, I got busted for burglarizing a grocery store. At 17, I should have been charged as a juvenile, but they charged me as an adult. I was out on probation in 1967 when I heard about Martin Luther King Jr.'s assassination while in jail. After a few months, I went to a party and got busted for burglarizing the Burnt River Liquor Store. I didn't think much of it at the time—I didn't even think I'd be found guilty. I went home, but they came after me. There was a car chase, and I eventually got caught. I ran up a hill, but they caught me and brought me back down. I went to jail for the Burnt River Liquor Store burglary and for not reporting it.

At the time, I had over 50 traffic tickets. They took me to traffic court first, where I went before a judge named Robin, who was blind. I started laughing, and the judge asked why I was laughing. Someone explained that I had over 57 traffic tickets, but the judge dismissed the charges. It was a strange moment—justice served by a blind judge.

When I was in jail in 1966 and the first part of 1967, I helped a guy named Jesse Phillips escape. Jesse was black, and his accomplice, Lauren Cunningham, was white. Back then, racism wasn't as big of a deal among us convicts—we just talked to each other like regular people. Jesse asked Lauren for a favor, and we set up the escape. Afterward, the authorities interrogated all the prisoners. When they got to me, I told them I was sleeping. I didn't rat on Jesse, and he knew it. That's why I sailed through prison—people saw I wasn't going to give anyone up. I was just trying to do my time and get out.

Later, I went to a party and got busted again. They took me to jail for the burglary, and that's when the Kidwell came into the picture. Everyone said he'd get off, but I thought, "No, this is justice. Justice should be served." They convicted him and sentenced him to life in prison. Two weeks later, I read in the paper that his case was overturned, and he got a reduced sentence of 5 to 20 years. He ended up serving only three years. Meanwhile, I went to prison with him after he got a shot of sodium amytal. I didn't get any such treatment.

When I got to prison, I hit the main line, while he went to protective custody. A few weeks later, they put him in a mobile home outside the prison. He lived there, working with the secretaries up front. When I heard about it, I looked out the window and saw him living in luxury. I thought, "This isn't justice. It's just us." That's how I got the name for my first book. Just us by Nobody. It is for sale on Amazon.

One day, I was "skating" (not where I was supposed to be) and got into an argument with a guard. A lieutenant came out, and I told him what I thought of the justice system. They took me to the hole, and one of the guards said something like, "It is the best system in the world." I told them what they could do with their criminal justice system. Another guard said, "They would kill Kidwell. I said don't you think they will kill me to?" I was just a young kid, and they didn't care about my welfare. They just wanted to make sure the guy in the mobile home was comfortable.

When I Was 25 Years Old:

This story takes place when I was about 25. I got arrested on a murder charge but was acquitted. However, they extradited me back to Colorado on a governor's warrant. I went before a judge, and the cop testified against me. The judge asked the cop for evidence, and the cop said, "I don't know anything about this case, but another officer said that another officer said that another officer said he's involved somehow." They bound me over on fifth-hand hearsay. At the preliminary hearing, the victim said, "He's not the one who robbed me," but the cop insisted I was guilty based on a photo lineup.

I know how they operate. Sometimes, they use photos where mine and Larry's pictures are 3x5, while everyone else's are 1x2. Who do you think they're going to pick? This kind of thing happens all the time in the American justice system. People don't want to believe it, but it's true.

Eventually, I want this story to reach Joe Biden and others in power. I'll say, "Kidwell got a shot of sodium amytal. Maybe everyone should get a shot of sodium amytal for arraignment. All you'd need is an email, fax, tweet, or message on my answering service. Then, we could go to the drugstore and get a shot. No shot, no justice, no peace." That's the deal. It's prejudice, plain and simple. Clown them—that's what I plan to do. That's why I'm telling this fifth-way hearsay story.

The troubling legacy of Martin Luther King

Newly-released documents reveal the full extent of the FBI's surveillance of the civil rights leader Dr Martin Luther King in the mid-1960s. They expose in graphic detail the FBI's intense focus on King's extensive extramarital sexual relationships with dozens of women, and also his presence in a Washington hotel room when a friend, a Baptist minister, allegedly raped one of his "parishioners", while King "looked on, laughed and offered advice". The FBI's tape recording of that criminal assault still exists today, resting under court seal in a National Archives vault. The FBI documents also reveal how its Director, J. Edgar Hoover, authorized top Bureau officials to send Dr King a tape recording of his sexual activities along with an anonymous message encouraging him to take his own life.

The complete transcripts and surviving recordings are not due to be released until 2027 but when they are made fully available a painful historical reckoning concerning King's personal conduct seems inevitable.

The **Chappaquiddick incident** occurred on Chappaquiddick Island, Massachusetts, United States, sometime around midnight between July 18 and 19, 1969, when United States Senator Ted

Kennedy drove his car off a narrow bridge, causing it to overturn in Poucha Pond. The crash resulted in the death (by suffocation) of his 28-year-old passenger, Mary JoKopechne, who was trapped inside the vehicle.

Kennedy left a party on Chappaquiddick Island, off the eastern end of Martha's Vineyard, at11:15 p.m. Friday July 18. He later stated that his intent was to immediately take Kopechneto a ferry landing and return to Edgartown, but that he accidentally made a wrong turn onto a dirt road leading to a one-lane bridge. After his car skidded off the bridge into the pond, Kennedy swam free, and maintained that he tried to rescue Kopechne from the submerged car but could not. Kopechne's death could have happened any time between about11:30 p.m. Friday and 1 a.m. Saturday, as an off-duty deputy sheriff stated he saw a car matching Kennedy's license plate at 12:40 a.m. Kennedy left the scene and did not report the accident to police until after 10 a.m. Saturday. Meanwhile, a diver recovered Kopechne's body from Kennedy's car shortly before 9 a.m. Saturday.

At a court hearing on July 25, Kennedy pleaded guilty to a charge of leaving the scene of an accident and received a two-month suspended jail sentence. In a televised statement that same evening, Kennedy said that his conduct immediately after the accident had "made no sense to me at all" and that he regarded his failure to report the accident immediately as" in defensible". A January 5, 1970, judicial inquest concluded that Kennedy and Kopechne had not intended to take the ferry, and that Kennedy had intentionally turned toward the bridge, operating his vehicle negligently if not recklessly and at too high a speed for the hazard which the bridge posed in the dark. The judge stopped short of recommending charges, and a grand jury convened on April 6, returning no indictments. On May 27, a Registry of Motor Vehicles hearing resulted in Kennedy's driver's license being suspended for sixteen months after the accident.

The Chappaquiddick incident became a national news item and influenced Kennedy's decision not to run for president in 1972 and 1976, Later it was said to have undermined his chances of ever becoming president. Kennedy ultimately decided to enter the 1980 Democratic presidential primaries, but earned only 37.6% of the vote and lost the nomination to incumbent U.S. President Jimmy Carter.

Claudine Longet Killed A Beloved Olympian 'By Accident' — And Spent Only 30 Days In Jail For It

A successful actress and singer, Claudine Longet became infamous after she shot skier Spider Sabich to death inside their Aspen, Colorado home on March 21, 1976.

Aspen, Colorado in 1976 was a fun, wealthy, and picturesque town. But all of that changed when singer Claudine Longet was arrested for shooting her boyfriend, beloved Olympian Vladimir "Spider" Sabich, to death.

Sabich was an adored athlete at the peak of his skiing career while Longet was a divorcé with a dwindling résumé. Rumors swirled that Sabich was even planning to leave her.

But the jury wasn't totally convinced.

"I wouldn't want her to go to prison, heavens no," said 27-year-old juror Daniel DeWolfe. "By no means is she the type of person who should be in jail. I don't think she's a threat to society."

After the four-day trial, jurors deliberated for a few hours before finding her guilty of criminally negligent homicide.

She was sentenced to 30 days of her choosing in prison and a $250 fine.

Patricia Campbell Hearst (born February 20, 1954) is the granddaughter of American publishing magnate William Randolph Hearst. She first became known for the events following her 1974 kidnapping by the Symbionese Liberation Army. She was found and arrested 19 months after being abducted, by which time she was a fugitive wanted for serious crimes committed with members of the group. She was held in custody, and there was speculation before trial that her family's resources would enable her to avoid time in prison.

At her trial, the prosecution suggested that Hearst had joined the Symbionese Liberation Army of her own volition. However, she testified that she had been raped and threatened with death while held captive. In 1976, she was convicted for the crime of bank robbery and sentenced to 35 years in prison, later reduced to seven years. Her sentence was commuted by President Jimmy Carter, and she was later pardoned by President Bill Clinton.

President Richard Nixon and Impeachable Offenses

The impeachment investigation and ensuing resignation of President Richard Nixon stands out as a profoundly important experience informing the standard for the impeachment of presidents. Although President Nixon was never impeached by the House or subjected to a trial in the Senate, his conduct exemplifies for many authorities, scholars, and the general public the paradigmatic case of impeachable behavior in a President.

Less than two years after a landslide reelection as President, Richard Nixon resigned following the House Judiciary Committee's adoption of three articles of impeachment against him. The circumstances surrounding the impeachment of President Nixon were sparked on June 17, 1972, by the arrest of five men for breaking into the Democratic National Headquarters at the Watergate Hotel and Office Building. The arrested men were employed by the Committee to Re-Elect the President (CRP), a campaign organization formed to support President Nixon's reelection.

In the early summer of 1973, Attorney General Elliot Richardson appointed Archibald Cox as a special prosecutor to investigate the connection between the five burglars and CRP. Likewise, the Senate Select Committee on Presidential Campaign Activities initiated its own investigation. After President Nixon fired various staffers allegedly involved in covering up the incident, he spoke on national television disclaiming knowledge of the cover up. However, the investigations uncovered evidence that President Nixon was involved, that he illegally harassed his enemies through, among other things, the use of tax audits, and that the men arrested for the Watergate break-in—the "plumbers unit," because they were used to "plug leaks" considered damaging to the Nixon Administration—

had committed burglaries before. Eventually a White House aide revealed that the President had a tape recording system in his office, raising the possibility that many of Nixon's conversations about the Watergate incident were recorded.

The President refused to hand over such tapes to the special prosecutor or Congress. In his capacity as special prosecutor, Cox then subpoenaed tapes of conversations in the Oval Office on Saturday, October 20, 1973. This sparked the sequence of events commonly known as the Saturday Night Massacre. In response to the subpoena, President Nixon ordered Attorney General Elliot Richardson to fire Special Prosecutor Cox. Richardson refused and resigned. Nixon ordered Deputy Attorney General William D. Ruckelshaus to fire the special prosecutor, but Ruckelshaus also refused to do so and resigned. Solicitor General Robert Bork, in his capacity as Acting Attorney General, then fired the special prosecutor. Nixon eventually agreed to deliver some of the subpoenaed tapes to the judge supervising the grand jury. The Justice Department appointed Leon Jaworski to replace Cox as special prosecutor.

The House Judiciary Committee began an official investigation of the Watergate issue and commenced impeachment hearings in April 1974. On March 1, 1974, a grand jury indicted seven individuals connected to the larger Watergate investigation and named the President as an unindicted coconspirator. On April 18, a subpoena was issued, upon the motion of the special prosecutor, by the United States District Court for the District of Columbia requiring the production of tapes and various items relating to meetings between the President and other individuals. Following a challenge to the subpoena in district court, the Supreme Court reviewed the case. On July 24, 1974, the Supreme Court affirmed the district court's order.

In late July, following its investigation and hearings, the House Judiciary Committee voted to adopt three articles of impeachment against President Nixon. The first impeachment article alleged that the President obstructed justice by attempting to impede the investigation into the Watergate break-in. The second charged the

President with abuse of power for using federal agencies to harass his political enemies and authorizing burglaries of private citizens who opposed the President. The third article accused the President of refusing to cooperate with the Judiciary Committee's investigation.

The Committee considered but rejected two proposed articles of impeachment. The first rejected article concerned receiving compensation in the form of government expenditures at his private properties in California and Florida—which allegedly constituted an emolument from the United States in violation of Article II, Section, 1, Clause 7 of the Constitution—and tax evasion. Those Members opposed to the portion of the charge alleging receipt of federal funds argued that most of the President's expenditures were made pursuant to a request from the Secret Service; that there was no direct evidence the President knew at the time that the source of these funds was public, rather than private; and that this conduct failed to rise to the level of an impeachable offense. Some Members opposed to the tax evasion charge argued that the evidence was insufficient to impeach; others that tax fraud is not the type of behavior "at which the remedy of impeachment is directed."

The second rejected article accused the President of concealing from Congress the bombing operations in Cambodia during the Vietnam conflict. This article was rejected for two primary reasons: some Members thought the President was performing his constitutional duty as Commander in Chief and Congress was given sufficient notice of these operations.

President Nixon resigned on August 9, 1974, before the full House voted on the articles. The lessons and standards established by the Nixon impeachment investigation and resignation are disputed. On the one hand, the behavior alleged in the *approved* articles against President Nixon is arguably a "paradigmatic" case of impeachment, constituting actions that are almost certainly impeachable conduct for the President.

On the other hand, the significance of the House Judiciary Committee's rejection of certain impeachment articles is unclear. In particular, whether conduct considered unrelated to the performance of official duties, such as the rejected article alleging tax evasion, can constitute an impeachable offense for the President is disputed. During the subsequent impeachment of President Bill Clinton, for example, the majority and minority reports of the House Judiciary Committee concerning the Committee's impeachment recommendation took different views on when conduct that might traditionally be viewed as private or unrelated to the functions of the presidency constituted an impeachable offense.

The House Judiciary Committee report that recommended articles of impeachment argued that perjury by the President was an impeachable offense, even if committed with regard to matters outside his official duties. In contrast, the minority views contained in the report argued that impeachment was reserved for "conduct that constitutes an egregious abuse or subversion of the powers of the executive office." The minority noted that the Judiciary Committee had rejected an article of impeachment against President Nixon alleging that he committed tax fraud, primarily because that "related to the President's private conduct, not to an abuse of his authority as President."

At 12:45 a.m. on March 3, 1991, robbery parolee Rodney G. King stops his car after leading police on a nearly 8-mile pursuit through the streets of Los Angeles, California. The chase began after King, who was intoxicated, was caught speeding on a freeway by a California Highway Patrol cruiser but refused to pull over. Los Angeles Police Department (LAPD) cruisers and a police helicopter joined the pursuit, and when King was finally stopped by Hansen Dam Park, several police cars descended on his white Hyundai. Go to Los Angeles, California they will treat you like a king, Rodney King.

Attica Prison Riot

The **Attica Prison riot** took place at the state prison in Attica, New York; it started on September 9, 1971, and ended on September 13 with the highest number of fatalities in the history of United States prison uprisings. Of the 43 men who died (33 inmates and 10 correctional officers and employees), all but one guard and three inmates were killed by law enforcement gunfire when the state retook control of the prison on the final day of the uprising. The Attica Uprising has been described as a historic event in the prisoners' rights movement.

Prisoners revolted to seek better living conditions and political rights, claiming that they were treated as beasts. On September 9, 1971, 1,281 of the approximately 2,200 men incarcerated in the Attica Correctional Facility rioted and took control of the prison, taking 42 staff hostage. During the four days of negotiations, authorities agreed to 28 of the prisoners' demands, but did not accept the demand for the removal of Attica's warden or to allow the inmates complete amnesty from criminal prosecution for the prison takeover. By order of Governor Nelson Rockefeller (after consultation with President Richard M. Nixon), armed corrections officers and state and local police were sent in to regain control of the prison. By the time they stopped firing, at least 39 people were dead: 10 correctional officers and civilian employees and 29 inmates, with nearly all killed by law enforcement gunfire. Law enforcement subjected many of the survivors to various forms of torture, including sexual violence.

Rockefeller had refused to go to the prison or meet with prisoners. After the uprising was suppressed, he falsely stated that the prisoners "carried out the cold-blood killings they had threatened from the outset". Medical examiners confirmed that all but the deaths of one officer and three inmates were caused by law enforcement gunfire. The *New York Times* writer Fred Ferretti said the rebellion concluded in "mass deaths that four days of taut negotiations had sought to avert."

As a result of the rebellion, the New York Corrections Department made changes in prisons to satisfy some of the prisoners' demands, reduce tension in the system, and prevent such incidents in the future. While there were improvements to prison conditions in the years immediately following the uprising, many of these improvements were reversed in the 1980s and 1990s. Attica remains one of the most infamous prison riots to have occurred in the United States.

The **New Mexico State Penitentiary riot**, which took place on February 2 and 3, 1980, at the Penitentiary of New Mexico (PNM) south of Santa Fe, was the most violent prison riot in U.S. history. Inmates took complete control of the prison and twelve officers were taken hostage. Several inmates were killed by other prisoners, with some being tortured and mutilated because they had previously acted as informants for prison authorities. Police regained control of PNM 36 hours after the riots had begun. By then, thirty-three inmates had died and more than two hundred were treated for injuries. None of the twelve officers taken hostage were killed, but seven suffered serious injuries caused by beatings and rapes.

There had been riots at PNM before it moved in 1956, the first occurring on July 19, 1922, and the second on June 15, 1953.

Hostages taken

The riot began with many of the prisoners intoxicated from homemade liquor they brewed inside the prison. Inmate Gary Nelson, assigned to E2 bunk 2, heard the plan to jump the guards if they did not lock the door to the dorm during the 1:00 a.m. count.

The routine for the count began with two officers entering the dormitory. A third officer was given all the other officers' keys and locked the door to the dorm until the officers were ready to come out. The dayroom was 60 feet all the way down to the far side of the dorm.[19] The TV needed to be turned off and the dayroom locked. Because of overcrowding, the two officers went down two sides of a center aisle consisting of single beds the length of the dorm. As one officer looked down to the right between the rows of bunk beds, the other officer looked down to the left between the rows of bunks. At the last second, the shift commander entered E2 to help with the count. After he was let in, the officer outside the door did not latch it. The prisoners on the bunks by the door had to keep the door open, otherwise all they would accomplish was the taking of three officers locked in their own dorm.

On Saturday morning at 1:40 a.m., February 2, 1980, on cue, two prisoners in south side Dormitory E2 overpowered the officer before he closed the door. Including the officer manning the door, this meant the prisoners took four officers hostage. They also had escaped E2 dorm. They rushed out and overpowered the other officers engaged in shutting down the Cell Blocks at the south end of the prison. At this point the riot might have been contained if the grille to the south wing had been closed and locked. Officers Larry Mendoza and Antonio Vigil, who were eating breakfast in the officers' mess hall, heard men's voices in the main corridor. A prisoner in an officer's uniform was standing by the open grille, apparently guarding it. Approaching the grille marching north was a hallway filled with prisoners. The officers soon realized the vulnerability of the grille being open as this meant the path lay wide open for the inmates to attack the control center. They both ran to the control center and warned the officer of the situation. The north grille beside the control center had also routinely been left open most nights. The two officers took refuge in the north wing of the prison. The control center closed and locked the north grille behind them.

By 2:05 a.m. the inmates had gained complete control of the prison by smashing the supposedly bulletproof plate glass window of the control center with a heavy brass fire extinguisher. This gave them access to lock and door controls. However, since they did not know how to open the cell doors automatically from the control center, Cell Houses 1, 2, and 6 had to be opened manually.

Modern Day Kings

This is about the Biden Brand. And Hunter Biden and How he had gun charges and problems with the I.R.S. And how the government tried to hide this from the public By no charges brought before the whistle blowers came forward. And how Joe Bide pardoned him.

Joe Biden in the Hur report. Said he took files from the archives.

And gave them to his ghost writer. Who in turn gave him eight million dollars. This is all on tape but they are hiding it just like they hid the Martin Luther King tape.

Joe Biden Should have been arrested. Because there was probable cause and reasonable suspicion. That grand larceny and theft had been seen and admitted. No charges for Joe Biden. And Hur said he did not know if he could get a conviction

And let me tell you if that was anyone else you would have been charged. And if you were. blind, crippled or crazy. That would be determined at a later date. That is what they tell everyone else.

Joe Biden not only does he pardon his son. He also pardoned his brother, his wife and four other family members. And they have not been convicted of anything. You have to be a KING to do such things.

I have been hearing a lot about nobody is above the law. The nobodies are not above the law. But it seems to me that the some bodies are above the law.

Hunter Biden laptop controversy
Hunter Biden in 2014

In October 2020, a controversy arose involving a laptop that belonged to Hunter Biden. The owner of a Delaware computer shop, John Paul Mac Isaac, said that the laptop had been left by a man who identified himself as Hunter Biden. Mac Isaac also stated that he is legally blind and could not be sure whether the man was actually Hunter Biden. Three weeks before the 2020 United States presidential election, the New York Post published a front-page story that presented emails from the laptop, alleging they showed corruption by Joe Biden, the Democratic presidential nominee and Hunter Biden's father. According to the Post, the story was based on information provided to Rudy Giuliani, the personal attorney of incumbent president and candidate Donald Trump, by Mac Isaac. Forensic analysis later authenticated some of the emails from the laptop, including one of the two emails used by the Post in their initial reporting.

Shortly after the *Post* story broke, social media companies blocked links to it, while other news outlets declined to publish the story due to concerns about provenance and suspicions of Russian disinformation. On October 19, 2020, an open letter signed by 51 former US intelligence officials said that the laptop "has all the classic earmarks of a Russian information operation." However, by May 2023, no evidence had publicly surfaced to support suspicions that the laptop was part of a Russian disinformation scheme.

In December 2019, under the authority of a subpoena issued by a Wilmington grand jury, the FBI seized the laptop from Mac Isaac. FBI investigators handling Hunter Biden's laptop quickly concluded in 2019 "that the laptop was genuinely his and did not seem to have been tampered with or manipulated". In June 2024, federal prosecutors utilized the laptop as evidence as part of a criminal case against Hunter Biden, alongside testimony from an FBI agent involved in authenticating and investigating the laptop.[16]

The hard drive data had been shared with Trump advisor Steve Bannon before it became publicly known. Trump attempted to turn the story into an October surprise to hurt Joe Biden's campaign by falsely alleging that, while in office, Biden had acted corruptly regarding Ukraine to protect his son. A joint investigation by two Republican Senate committees released in September 2020 and a Republican House Oversight committee investigation released in April 2024 did not find wrongdoing by Joe Biden with regard to Ukraine and his son's business dealings there. PolitiFact wrote in June 2021 that the laptop did belong to Hunter Biden, but did not demonstrate wrongdoing by Joe Biden.

Starting in 2021, news outlets began to authenticate some of the contents of the laptop. In 2021, Politico verified two key emails used in the *Post's* initial reporting by cross-referencing emails with other datasets and contacting their recipients. CBS News published a forensic analysis which examined a "clean" copy of the data obtained directly from Mac Isaac. It concluded that the "clean" data, including over 120,000 emails, originated with Hunter Biden and had not been altered, while other copies circulated by

Republican operatives "could have been tampered with". Other outlets also verified portions of the data, while noting problems in fully authenticating the copies they had to work with.

Background

The media coverage of the laptop spurred speculation about the Biden–Ukraine conspiracy theory, which falsely alleged that then vice president Joe Biden acted in Ukraine to protect his son from a corruption investigation by Ukrainian Prosecutor General Viktor Shokin. On October 14, 2020, the *New York Post* published an article based on an email from the laptop about a purported meeting between then vice president Joe Biden and the Burisma advisor Vadym Pozharskyi. The Biden campaign denied Joe Biden had any meeting with Pozharskyi and said that if they had ever met, it would have been a brief encounter.[28] Witnesses at the dinner where they allegedly met said Joe Biden briefly passed by to see an old friend. The *Post* reported in its story that Pozharskyi declined to comment, and he did not comment to a *Politico* journalist who reported extensively on the story a year later.

The *Post* reported that the email was found in a cache of data extracted from the external hard drive of a laptop computer that belonged to Hunter Biden. The *Post* reported that the repair shop owner had made a copy of the external hard drive before it was seized by the US Federal Bureau of Investigation (FBI) and that the copy was later provided to the *Post* by Donald Trump's attorney, Rudy Giuliani. The subpoena to seize the laptop was issued by a grand jury on behalf of the US attorney's office in Wilmington, which was later reported to have been investigating Hunter Biden about lobbying and financial matters since at least 2018.

The veracity of the *Post*'s reporting was strongly questioned by many mainstream media outlets and analysts due to the initially unclear origin and chain of custody of the laptop and the provenance of its contents. Due to prior Russian influence campaigns during the 2016 election, particularly the release of documents obtained by Russian cyber attacks targeting John Podesta and the Democratic

National Committee, media outlets and intelligence officials also became suspicious of a possible disinformation campaign by Russian intelligence or its proxies. Analysts also suspected Russian involvement in the 2017 leaks of emails involving French president Emmanuel Macron two days before national elections, which contained fake emails mingled with genuine ones. Adding to concerns, Giuliani had met with Andrii Derkach, later confirmed to be a Russian agent,[31][32] while conducting opposition research against Joe Biden in Ukraine in 2019.

Special Counsel Robert Hur Testifies in House Hearing

Special counsel Robert Hur was questioned during a House hearing on President Biden's handling of classified documents. Read the transcript here.

Mr. Jordan (00:00):

Acting Chairman Comer and Ranking Member Raskin will be permitted to participate in today's hearing for the purposes of making opening statements and asking questions of the witness. They each will receive three minutes for an opening statement and five minutes to question the witness. The chair now recognizes himself for an opening statement. Robert Hur was appointed as special counsel on January 12, 2023. He had a fundamental question to address. Did Joe Biden unlawfully retain classified information? The answer, yes, he did. Page one of Mr. Hur's report, he says this, "Our investigation uncovered evidence that President Biden willfully retained and disclosed classified materials after his Vice Presidency when he was a private citizen." He further writes, "Mr. Biden willfully retained marked classified documents about Afghanistan and hand-written notes in his notebooks, which he stored in unsecured places in his home." Joe Biden kept classified information, and Joe Biden failed to store classified information properly.

Mr. Hur made these determinations after interviewing 147 witnesses. He examined seven million documents, including emails, text messages, photographs, videos, toll records, and other materials from both classified and unclassified sources. But there's more. Joe Biden not only kept information he wasn't allowed to keep, and he not only failed to secure that information properly, he also shared it with people who weren't allowed to see it. Shared that information with his ghost writer. And remember, this is information that only individuals with the security clearance are supposed to see. Mr. Hur told us on page 200 of his report that it's the kind of information that "risks serious damage to America's national security." What did Joe Biden have to say about all this? What was his explanation? On page 94 of Mr. Hur's report, Joe Biden said he took his notebooks with him after his Vice Presidency because "they're mine. And every President before me has done the same exact thing."

Never mind the fact that he had never been president when he took this information, but what comes through is Joe Biden felt he was entitled. You can almost hear it. You can feel the arrogance in this statement, "they're mine." But even with all that, Mr. Hur chose not to bring charges because "Mr. Biden would likely present himself to a jury, as he did in our interview of him, as a sympathetic, well-meaning elderly man with a poor memory." A forgetful old man who Mr. Hur said did not remember when he was Vice President, forgetting on the first day of the interview when his term ended, and forgetting on the second day of the interview when his term as Vice President began. Mr. Hur produced a 345-page report, but in the end, it boils down to a few key facts. Joe Biden kept classified information, Joe Biden failed to properly secure classified information, and Joe Biden shared classified information with people he wasn't supposed to. Joe Biden broke the law. Because he's a forgetful old man who would appear sympathetic to a jury, Mr. Hur chose not to bring charges. Mr. Hur, we think it's important that you be able to respond to President Biden's response to your report. We're going to play a short video of President Biden's press conference after your report was released because there's things in this press conference that the President of the United States says that are directly contradicted by what you found in your report. If we could play that video.

What a tangled web we weave when we practice to deceive.

Sir Walter Scott poem Marmion

Maybe what we should do as American citizens is give all of the following immunity to all crimes. The guards and police officers, judges and district attorneys, House and Congress. And the President of the United States and his family. They got immunity no matter. I think we should give immunity to the rich movie stars and professional athletes.

www.ingramcontent.com/pod-product-compliance
Lightning Source LLC
Chambersburg PA
CBHW031240120626
46545CB00003B/1203